HIDING IN THE
POLAR REGIONS

Deborah Underwood

www.raintreepublishers.co.uk
Visit our website to find out
more information about
Raintree books.

To order:
☏ Phone 0845 6044371
🖷 Fax +44 (0) 1865 312263
🖳 Email myorders@raintreepublishers.co.uk

Customers from outside the UK please telephone +44 1865 312262

Raintree is an imprint of Capstone Global Library Limited,
a company incorporated in England and Wales having
its registered office at 7 Pilgrim Street, London, EC4V 6LB
– Registered company number: 6695582

Edited by Rebecca Rissman and Nancy Dickmann
Designed by Joanna Hinton Malivoire
Picture research by Tracy Cummins
Originated by Capstone Global Library
Printed and bound in China by Leo Paper Products Ltd.

ISBN 978 0 431 00959 9 (hardback)
15 14 13 12 11
10 9 8 7 6 5 4 3 2 1

ISBN 978 1 406 22006 3 (paperback)
16 15 14 13 12
10 9 8 7 6 5 4 3 2 1

British Library Cataloguing in Publication Data
Underwood, Deborah.
   Hiding in the polar regions. -- (Creature camouflage)
   1. Animals--Polar regions--Juvenile literature.
   2. Camouflage (Biology)--Juvenile literature.
   I. Title II. Series
   591.4'72'0911-dc22

Acknowledgements
We would like to thank the following for permission to reproduce
photographs: FLPA pp. 6 (Hannu Hautala), 7 (Imagebroker/
Jonathan Carlile) 15, 16 (Terry Whittaker); Getty Images pp. 8
(Johnny Johnson), 27 (Michael S. Quinton), 28 (Joseph Van Os),
29 (Doug Allan); naturepl.com pp. 11, 12 (© Warwick Sloss), 19, 20
(© Tom Mangelsen), 21, 22 (© Ian McCarthy); Photolibrary p. 9
(Owen Newman); Shutterstock pp. 4 (© Map Resources), 5
(© YellowSummer), 13, 14 (© Mark Yarchoan), 17, 18 (© Vladimir
Melnik), 23, 24 (© Morten Hilmer); Visuals Unlimited, Inc. pp. 10
(© Rick Poley), 25, 26 (© Joe McDonald).

Cover image of an arctic fox used with permission of Getty
Images (Paul Nicklen).

We would like to thank Michael Bright for his invaluable help in
the preparation of this book.

Contents

Some words are printed in bold, **like this**. You can find out what they mean by looking in the glossary.

What are polar regions like?

Polar regions are cold, icy places. Earth's polar regions are the Arctic and the Antarctic. The Sun's rays are not strong in polar regions. This means the weather is cold.

The places at the top and bottom of this map are the coldest.

Pieces of ice float in Arctic seas.

Parts of polar regions are icy or snowy all the time. The edges of polar regions have warmer temperatures. There, the snow and ice melt in summer.

Living in polar regions

Many animals could not live in polar regions. Polar animals must live in very cold weather. How do they **survive**?

Parts of polar regions stay dark for months at a time!

A thick layer of fat helps keep a walrus warm in the Arctic.

Polar animals have special **features** that help them to **survive** in the cold. These features are called **adaptations**.

What is camouflage?

Camouflage is an **adaptation** that helps animals hide. The colour of an animal's skin, fur, or feathers may match the things around it.

Reindeer have brown coats that help them **blend in** with the things around them.

Camouflage helps keep young animals like these fox cubs safe.

Many polar animals change colour. They turn white in winter to hide in the snow. In the summer, they grow dark fur or feathers. This helps them to hide in rocks and earth.

Predators are animals that eat other animals. **Prey** animals are animals that predators eat. **Camouflage** helps both types of animals hide from each other.

Eggs can be camouflaged, too. These eggs look like pebbles.

Find the polar animals

CAMOUFLAGED

Polar bear

Polar bears live only in the Arctic. Their white fur **blends in** with snow and ice. It helps them hide when they hunt for food.

Polar bears are very good swimmers.
They have a thick layer of fat called
blubber. The blubber keeps the bears
warm in the icy Arctic water.

Ptarmigan

A ptarmigan is a type of bird. Ptarmigans have dark feathers in summer. Females make nests on the ground. Their colour helps them hide from foxes and owls.

CAMOUFLAGED

In winter, snow covers the ground. The ptarmigans lose their dark feathers. They grow white feathers. This helps them to **blend in** with the snow.

Arctic hare

Arctic hares change colour, too. Their fur is snowy white in winter. They grow grey or brown fur in summer. Their fur colour helps them to hide from **predators**, such as wolves and foxes.

CAMOUFLAGED

Arctic hares have another **adaptation** that helps them to **survive** in the cold. Animals lose heat through their ears. Arctic hares have short ears. This helps them stay warm.

REVEALED

Harp seal

Some **predators** hunt young **prey** animals because young prey are weaker. Young harp seals have fluffy, white fur. This helps the young seals **blend in** with the ice.

As harp seals grow, their fur turns grey and black. Adult seals spend most of their lives in the water. Their grey fur is better **camouflage** in the water than white fur would be.

Ermine

Ermine are a type of weasel. Their fur is dark on the top parts of their bodies. The underneath parts are white. The tips of their tails are black.

Ermine that live in very cold places turn white in the winter. Can you guess why? But the tips of their tails stay black all the year round!

REVEALED

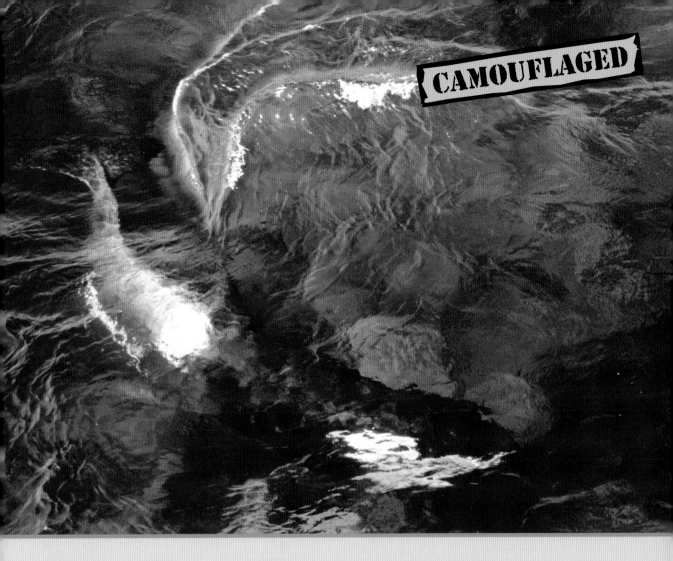

Orca

Orcas are also known as killer whales. You would think that their black and white colour might make them easy to see. But it actually helps them hide in the water!

An animal looking down in the water may not spot an orca. Its black back can **blend in** with the ocean floor. An animal looking up might think the orca's white belly looks like sunlight on the ocean.

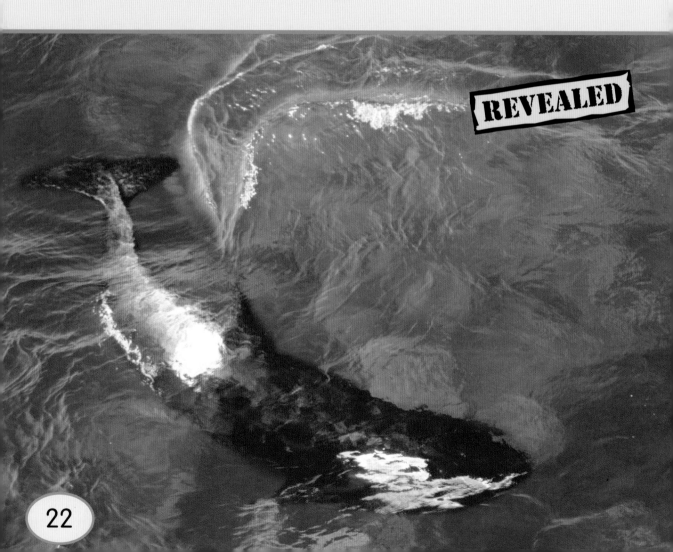

REVEALED

Arctic fox

Arctic foxes have brown or grey coats in summer. They can hide in soil. In winter, their coats turn snowy white. The foxes can hide in snow. Blending in helps them creep up on other animals as they hunt.

CAMOUFLAGED

Arctic foxes hunt for small animals, birds, and fish. Sometimes a fox will follow a polar bear. It hopes to eat the bear's leftovers! The fox's coat helps it to hide so the bear doesn't eat it.

REVEALED

CAMOUFLAGED

Snowy owl

Snowy owls live in the Arctic. Sometimes they travel south to find food. The owls' **camouflage** helps to hide them from foxes and wolves. It also helps the owls to hide as they wait for **prey**.

Snowy owls eat small animals, such as mice and lemmings. The owls are very good at hearing. They can hear other animals moving beneath the snow!

REVEALED

These Dall sheep would be camouflaged in the snow – if it weren't for their big horns!

Camouflage helps to hide some polar animals when they hunt. It helps hide other animals from **predators**. Camouflage helps polar animals to **survive** in their cold surroundings.

Animals that stand out

Emperor penguins do not need to hide when they are on land. No land animals hunt them. Penguins only hunt in the sea.

Emperor penguins are easy to spot when they stand on the Antarctic ice.

The penguins' dark backs and light bellies help them to hide in the water.

The penguins' colours help to hide them when they swim in the sea. Like orcas, their black backs and white bellies make them hard to see underwater.

Glossary

adaptation feature that helps an animal survive in its surroundings

blend in matches well with the things around it

camouflage adaptation that helps an animal blend in with its surroundings

feature special part of an animal

predator animal that eats other animals

prey animal that other animals eat

survive stay alive

Find out more

Books to read

Essential Habitats: Polar Habitats, Barbara Taylor (Ticktock Media Ltd., 2009)

Introducing Habitats: The Arctic Habitat, Molly Aloian (Crabtree Publishing, 2006)

Saving Wildlife: Polar Animals, Sonya Newland (Franklin Watts, 2010)

Websites

www.antarctica.ac.uk/about_antarctica/wildlife/index.php
Antarctic wildlife information from the British Antarctic Survey.

www.bbc.co.uk/nature/habitats/Polar_region
Visit this BBC website to find out more about polar regions and the animals that live there.

www.kids.nationalgeographic.com/Photos/Arctic-animals
Look at spectacular photographs of Arctic animals on the National Geographic website.

Index